This Book Belongs to

_____

To my sweet Mymy,
Thank you for being such an inspiration to
me since the day you were born.
Continue using that big imagination
of yours to create magic.
I love you,
Mommy

MILAH'S MAGICAL ADVENTURE
A Trip Around the Globe

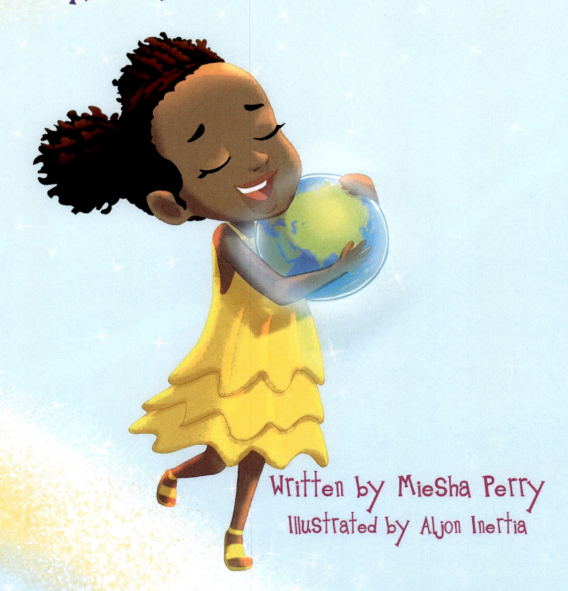

Written by MieSha Perry
Illustrated by Aljon Inertia

It was the first day of summer.
Milah awakens to the hot sun beaming through the window, feeling warm on her face.

She excitedly jumps out of bed
and quickly gets ready for her day.

Following the smell of a delicious breakfast,
Milah finds her mom in the kitchen.

"Good morning, Mom," says Milah.
"What adventures are we going on today?"

"We can go on any adventure you like,
but not until after lunch," replies Milah's mom.

"Lunch?" Milah shouts. "It is only eight o'clock in the morning! Lunch will take ages!"

"Sorry, honey. You will just have to use that BIG imagination of yours until then."

After breakfast, Milah searches the house for something fun to do.
She stumbles across a new, shiny globe.

Milah spins the globe as fast as she can and whispers,
"I wish you were magic so that you could take me anywhere in the world."

Suddenly, Milah hears someone say, "Hi. I'm Orby. I would love to explore all of my continents with you."

Milah looks up and sees the globe is alive. She is shocked that her wish came true!

"Hello, Orby. It is nice to meet you, but what is a continent?"

"I am glad you asked," he says. "Continents are very large landmasses found on Earth. If you look closely at me, you will find that I have seven continents."

Milah studies the globe. She finds each one, then says, "I see Asia, Africa, North America, South America, Antarctica, Europe, and Australia."

Orby says, "Correct! Those are the seven continents. Would you like to visit them?"

Excited to learn more about the continents, Milah asks, "How will we get there?"

"Well, it's quite simple," he says.
"All you must do is repeat this song after me."

Orby sings, "Come on, friends, let's explore!
Close your eyes so that you can see more.
Spin me fast and just believe how far your imagination
can take you in 1, 2, 3!!"

Milah sings, and Orby says,
"Welcome to Asia, the largest and most populated continent of them all.
Asia is the home of Mount Everest, the tallest mountain on Earth.
It will take someone at least two months to climb to the top.
You can also find Giant Pandas roaming in the forest around Asia."

"How tall is Mount Everest?" asks Milah.

"Mount Everest peck is at 29,029 feet", responds Orby.

"That is enormous," Milah says

"It is, but we need to keep going," says Orby. "So, repeat after me. Come on, friends, let's explore! Close your eyes so that you can see more. Spin me fast and just believe how far your imagination can take you in 1, 2, 3!!"

Milah spins the globe and Orby says,
"Welcome to Africa, the second largest and second most populated continent.
Africa is proudly known as the continent where humans originated.
It is also the home of the Sahara Desert,
which is the largest hot desert in the world.
You can find camels traveling for days with no food or water in Africa."

A little confused by what a desert was, Milah asked Orby to explain.

"Deserts are areas of land that are dry, meaning it doesn't rain much." Orby explains.

Let's keep going," says Orby. "So, repeat after me.
Come on, friends, let's explore. Close your eyes so that you can see more.
Spin me fast and just believe how far your
imagination can take you in 1, 2, 3!!"

Milah does, and Orby says, "Welcome to North America, the third-largest and fourth most populated continent on Earth. North America is home to Lake Superior, which is the largest freshwater lake in the world. You can find the American alligator swimming around the freshwater lakes and swamps in some areas of North America."

"What do American alligators eat?" asks Milah

"American alligators are carnivores and will eat fish, snakes, and birds, to name a few," explains Orby. "People stay away from those hungry animals."

Milah excitedly spins the globe, and Orby says, "Welcome to South America, the fourth-largest and fifth most populated continent. South America is the home of Angel Falls, the highest waterfall in the world. South America is also known as 'the Bird Continent' because you can find many different species there, including toucans."

"How tall is Angel Falls?" asked Milah.

Angel falls stands at 3,212 feet, which is so high that the water turns into mist before hitting the stream below it on warmer days." Orby explains.

"That is so cool!" Milah says.

"It is, but we need to keep going, says Orby.
"So, repeat after me. Come on, friends, let's explore.
Close your eyes so that you can see more.
Spin me fast and just believe how far your imagination
can take you in 1, 2, 3!!"

Milah spins again and Orby says,
"Welcome to Antarctica, the fifth-largest continent. Because it is a landmass covered by ice, scientists only visit it to do research for short periods of time. Antarctica is considered a desert, and it is the coldest, driest, and windiest continent of them all. It is the home of the South Pole. You can find penguins sliding across the ice in Antarctica."

"How do Penguins stay warm if Antarctica is the coldest continent?" ask Milah.

Penguins have thick skin, and they huddle closely together to keep warm." Orby explains.

"So, they take care of each other?" Milah asked.

Yes, they do, and we need to keep going," says Orby. "So, repeat after me. Come on, friends, let's explore. Close your eyes so that you can see more. Spin me fast and just believe how far your imagination can take you in 1, 2, 3!!"

Milah does, and Orby says,
"Welcome to Europe, the second smallest and third most populated continent.
Europe is the home of Mount Etna, one of the most active volcanoes in the world.
You can find reindeer roaming freely through the countrysides in Europe."

"What is an active volcano?" asks Milah.

"There a three types of volcanoes; active, dormant, and extinct," explains Orby.
"An active volcano means it will likely erupt again, dormant means it might erupt again but hasn't in a long time, and extinct means it will never erupt again."

"You're asking such good questions, Milah,
but we should keep going," says Orby.
"So, repeat after me. Come on, friends, let's explore.
Close your eyes so that you can see more.
Spin me fast and just believe how far your imagination
can take you in 1, 2, 3!!"

Milah spins, and Orby says,
"Welcome to Australia, the smallest and least populated continent of them all.
Australia is the home of Ayers Rock, the largest stand-alone rock in the world.
You can find kangaroos hopping across the roads,
with their babies in their pouches, in Australia."

"Wow, that's amazing," says Milah.
"I have seen some amazing new things during
our adventure, today, Orby!
I can't wait to tell my mom!" Milah says, excitedly.

About the Author

Miesha Perry is the mother of one creative little girl who has a big imagination. She is a full-time social worker whose focus is on ensuring families have the tools to raise children in healthy, loving environments.

Miesha lives every day, being inspired, and completing acts of service. She also volunteers as a youth cheer coach, and she adores her Lady Falcons.

Miesha knew that her love for children and her dedication to their development would bring her to write a children's book one day. Inspired by her daughter and realizing the importance of creating something special for children to enjoy was essential to Miesha. Her book, Milah's Magical Adventure: A Trip Around the Globe, brought to life her dream of leaving a legacy for the next generation.

The first in a series, this book shows children how using their imagination can make learning fun while teaching geography and fun facts about each of the world continents.

Visit www.milahsmagicaladventures.com

About the Illustrator

Aljon Inertia specializes in creating beautiful, one-of-a-kind illustrations for children's books. He started drawing at the age of 18 after being diagnosed with heart enlargement. While on bed rest and recovering, Aljon fell in love with the art of illustration and promised to pursue his career as an artist/illustrator.

His goal and purpose in life are to bring his passion for illustration to children's books that speak to good morals and values while providing lessons to today's youth. His colorful illustrations bring engagement to the author's content, so the story comes alive on the book's pages.

In 2019, Aljon, by invitation, attended Book Expo in New York to showcase his work, which he creates in his private studio in the Philippines. His creative illustrations are published in children's books worldwide.

Follow Aljon on Instagram @inertiaillustrator

COMING SOON

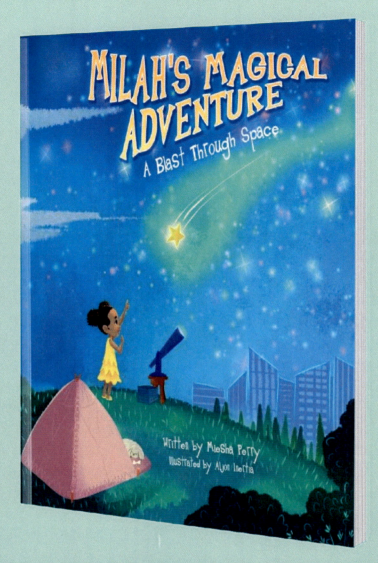

Milah is a young girl with a big imagination and a love for learning.

One night while gazing at the night sky through her telescope, she saw her very own shooting star. Milah took a moment, closed her eyes, and made an extraordinary wish.

With that wish, her shooting star comes to life. Together, they go on a magical adventure.

On their journey, Milah and "Nebi" take a blast through space, exploring the eight planets revolving around the sun in our Solar System. Milah learns fun facts about what makes each planet unique, including its size, distance from the sun, how many moons each one has, and more!

Come on along for this fantastic and MAGICAL learning adventure!

© 2020 Miesha Perry

© 2020 Illustrated by Aljon Inertia

Published in the United States of America
All rights reserved worldwide.
Authentic Endeavors Publishing /Book Endeavors
Clarks Summit PA 18411

No part of this book may be reproduced by any mechanical, photographic or electronic process, or in the form of an audio or digital recording, nor may it be stored in any retrieval system, transmitted or otherwise, be copied for public or private use – other than for fair use as brief quotation embodied in articles and review - without prior written permission of the author, illustrators or publisher.
This publication is a work of fiction. Names, characters, businesses, places, events, and incidents are either the products of the author's imagination or used in a fictitious manner. Any resemblance to actual persons, living or dead or actual events or places is purely coincidental.

ISBN: 978-0-9982105-8-2
Library of Congress Control Number: 2020924463

Made in the USA
Monee, IL
19 January 2021